D1528914

Soccer Star Ronaldinho

Speeding Star
Keep Boys Reading!

John Albert Torres

Speeding Star, an imprint of Enslow Publishers, Inc.

Library of Congress Cataloging-in-Publication Data
Torres, John Albert.
Soccer star Ronaldinho / John Albert Torres.
pages cm. — (Goal! Latin stars of soccer)
Includes bibliographical references and index.
Summary: "Brazilian soccer star Ronaldinho became a star at a young age and has grown to become a superstar on the biggest stage. In this sports biography, follow Ronaldinho on his journey to becoming an international soccer star"—Provided by publisher.
ISBN 978-1-62285-223-9
1. Ronaldinho, 1980-—Juvenile literature. 2. Soccer players—Brazil—Biography—Juvenile literature. I. Title.
GV942.7.R6258T67 2014
796.334092—dc23
[B]
2013014574

Future Editions:
Paperback ISBN: 978-1-62285-177-5
EPUB ISBN: 978-1-62285-178-2
Single-User PDF ISBN: 978-1-62285-179-9
Multi-User PDF ISBN: 978-1-62285-180-5

Printed in the United States of America
112013 Bang Printing, Brainerd, Minn.
10 9 8 7 6 5 4 3 2 1

To Our Readers: We have done our best to make sure all Internet addresses in this book were active and appropriate when we went to press. However, the author and the Publisher have no control over, and assume no liability for, the material available on those Internet sites or on other Web sites they may link to. Any comments or suggestions can be sent by e-mail to comments@speedingstar.com or to the address below.

Speeding Star
Box 398, 40 Industrial Road
Berkeley Heights, NJ 07922
USA
www.speedingstar.com

Enslow Publishers, Inc., is committed to printing our books on recycled paper. The paper in every book contains 10% to 30% post-consumer waste (PCW). The cover board on the outside of each book contains 100% PCW. Our goal is to do our part to help young people and the environment too!

Photo Credits: ©AP Images/Ahn Young-joon, p. 23; ©AP Images/Bernat Armangue, p. 27; ©AP Images/Daniel Jayo, p. 4; ©AP Images/Daniel Maurer, p. 32; ©AP Images/Eduardo Di Baia, p. 40; ©AP Images/Fabio Motta/Agencia Estado, p. 24; AP Images/Francois Mori, p. 20; ©AP Images/Jae C. Hong, p. 35; ©AP Images/Juan Karita, p. 7; ©AP Images/Luca Bruno, p. 33; ©AP Images/Manu Fernandez, p. 36; ©AP Images/Marcos de Paula/Agencia Estado, p. 11; ©AP Images/Michael Dwyer, p. 31; ©AP Images/Michel Euler, p. 13; ©AP Images/Michel Spingler, p. 19; ©AP Images/Nelson Antoine, p. 28; ©AP Images/Nick Wass, p. 8; ©AP Images/Oscar Hidalgo, p. 17; ©AP Images/Silvia Izquierdo, p. 25; ©AP Images/Thomas Kienzle, p. 14; ©AP Images/Uarlen Valerio/Agencia Estado, p. 43.

Cover Photo: ©AP Images/Andre Penner

CONTENTS

A young Ronaldinho jumps for joy after scoring his team's sixth goal against Venezuela in 1999.

chapter

1

What a Goal!

He might have been feeling a bit shy but no one would have known it. The teenage soccer star came onto the soccer pitch late in the game as a substitute for Brazil's national team against rival country Venezuela.

At stake was the Copa de América, or America's Cup tournament.

Up until that point, this had been the biggest stage for the young player who had started playing soccer at the age of five.

What Ronaldinho did during his few minutes on the field of play would be a moment to be remembered forever by Brazilian soccer fans all over the world. It didn't matter that Brazil had a commanding lead over Venezuela on its way to a 7–0 victory.

It didn't matter that the goal came against a weaker team. No, what Ronaldinho did with the ball was nothing short of spectacular. And it would have been amazing regardless of the opponent.

He was just to the right of the penalty area arc facing the goal. With a smile on his face, Ronaldinho faked running forward, and the defender lurched back expecting a run toward the goal. But just as quickly as he started, Ronaldinho stopped in his tracks. He was about forty-five yards away from the goal. Then he placed his right foot over the ball and started gently pulling it back toward himself. He was hoping that the Venezuelan defender would follow the ball.

He did. The defender started closing in on Ronaldinho. As soon as the defender was very close, the Brazilian star did what he knew best. A master of ball control with little kicks, flicks, and touches, he squeezed his right foot under the ball and flicked it just over the oncoming player's shoulder.

Then Ronaldinho scooted left around the defender. This was confusing to the defender because most right-handed players would have tried to go right around the player. But Ronaldinho went left. He then controlled the ball right on his foot as it landed about thirty-five yards from the Venezuelan goalkeeper, who started moving toward the play to get in proper position. Another defender came flying in from the corner, but Ronaldinho's speed was too much.

He tapped and dribbled the ball ahead for a couple of steps and then unleashed a rocket of a shot past the keeper in to the far corner of the goal. It was an incredible goal. No one had ever seen someone so young control the ball as if he was merely toying with the other players, daring them to take it from him.

The youngster jumped high in the air and threw a fist in celebration. A wide, joyous smile came to his face. His teammates gathered around him and congratulated him on such a powerful scoring strike and incredible ball control.

When people say that Ronaldinho's career is nearing its end, he goes out and proves that he can still play like he is twenty years old.

Some soccer experts said the goal was more like a work of art that should be hung in an art gallery or museum somewhere. It lives forever on the Internet where millions of people have admired it.

If he did not know it yet, that was the moment that Ronaldinho became a star.

This was still years before he would grow his signature long hair, braided and bouncing behind him as he dominated the pitch. But even back then, even in 1999, Ronaldinho was very easy to spot on the soccer pitch because of the wide smile he always seemed to be wearing, no matter what the situation or the score.

Most players don't even attempt the bicycle kick, but Ronaldinho does whatever he must do to score for his team.

He was only nineteen years old, but the Brazilian media was already comparing him to Pelé, considered by many to be the greatest soccer player who ever lived.

While the comparisons were obviously a bit premature, expectations were already sky-high for the teenager. Only two years earlier, in 1997, he was a main part of the first Brazilian team to ever win the FIFA U-17 World Championship. This pits players younger than seventeen from all over the world against one another.

He had scored two goals in that tournament and was given the Bronze Ball Award as the best player on the team. He was immediately called up to help the U-20 team.

It would only be the start of things to come for the young footballer who would leave his mark on the game in the minds and memories of everyone who watched him play.

"I don't think anyone has played as beautifully as Ronaldinho," said fellow Brazilian soccer star Tinga, who is from the same city as Ronaldinho. "And at the same time he always did it with a smile on his face."

It was a smile that would carry him from poor, humble beginnings in a Brazilian port city, across the oceans to several continents and countries where he would land at the very top of the soccer world.

Growing Up

Ronaldo de Assis Moreira was born on March 21, 1980 in the southern Brazilian city of Porto Alegre. He would later be known simply as Ronaldinho, or little Ronaldo.

Translated into English, Porto Alegre means "Happy Port" or "Happy Harbor." It is one of the largest cities in Brazil with nearly 4.5 million people living there. Because the port city was founded in 1772 by Portuguese settlers who established a shipping center, many Europeans from Germany, Italy, Spain, and Poland settled in the city over the years.

That explains the diverse culture and the different styles of food, dress, and even architecture throughout the area. What's interesting is that even though Porto Alegre is near the ocean, the port itself is not. It sits at a place where five rivers come together and form a giant freshwater lake called Lagoa dos Patos that giant ships use to go from the ocean to the port.

The climate is subtropical, meaning that it is pretty hot and muggy just about all year round.

Ronaldinho's mother—Dona Miguelina Elói Assis dos Santos—used to work selling makeup and cosmetics. But she wanted more out of life. She wanted to help others, so she later studied to become a nurse. The boy's father—João de Assis Moreira—was a former professional soccer player who worked as a welder at the nearby shipyards.

Roberto, Ronaldinho's brother, also played professional soccer before becoming his younger brother's manager.

He still played soccer for a local club in their neighborhood of Villanova. But that is not surprising. In many Latin American countries, such as Brazil, just about everyone plays soccer. In fact, in Brazil many people refer to soccer as "the beautiful game." If baseball is the national pastime in the United States, then soccer is the national passion in Brazil.

Ronaldinho's older brother, Roberto de Assis Moreira, was also a professional soccer player known as Assis. It was as if Ronaldinho was born in a soccer world.

"I come from a family where soccer has always been very present," he says. "My uncles, my father, and my brother were all players. Living with that kind of background, I learned a great deal from them. I tried to devote myself to it more and more with the passage of time."

But even though it was Roberto who was very popular around the city as a well-known soccer player, the young Ronaldinho had only one idol as a little boy. It was his father and very little of it had to do with the sport they all loved so much.

He loved and was very close to his father for the life lessons he taught him. These lessons had nothing to do with soccer but more about becoming a man.

"He gave me some of the best advice I've ever had," Ronaldinho said. "Off the field he told me to do the right thing and be an honest, straight-up guy."

Of course, this was Brazil and somehow or other

The name Ronaldinho might mean "little Ronaldo," but when he is on the pitch, he is the biggest concern for his opponents.

just about every conversation or piece of advice would eventually end up about soccer.

"On the field, he told me to 'play soccer as simply as possible,'" Ronaldinho recounted. "He always said one of the most complicated things you can do is to play it simple."

Ronaldinho wasn't even five years old when he was given his very first soccer ball. From that instant it seemed as if the boy knew exactly what to do with it. Home videos of the young boy can be found on the Internet dribbling the ball and then balancing it on his head, back, and shoulders. It was clear that he was comfortable with the ball.

He was seven years old when he joined his first team in an organized soccer league. He had played a lot of soccer in

While it may look like his kicks are effortless, Ronaldinho has one of the hardest shots in all of soccer.

the streets and empty lots with his friends. So by the time he was on a real team in a youth league, he was already much better than the kids his age.

He was put on a team with older kids. Because he was youngest, he was also the smallest. That was the first time people began calling him Ronaldinho, or little Ronaldo.

"They always called me that when I was little because I was really small," he would later laugh.

The soccer field was in very poor shape. The only grass on the field was in the corner. There was only dirt and sand on most of the field. During that time, Ronaldinho and his friend also started playing another game or sport that is very similar to soccer. It is called futsal.

Futsal is played indoors and on hard surfaces like schoolyard playgrounds. It's played in a very small space with only five players per side. Because there is not a lot of open space, the best futsal players are the ones who have the best footwork, who can control the ball the best. The ball is also a little heavier than a traditional soccer ball.

"A lot of the moves I make originate from futsal," Ronaldinho said. "It's played in a very small space, and the ball control is different in futsal. And to this day my ball control is pretty similar to a futsal player's control."

Ronaldinho played futsal for fun. He never thought that it would help make him a great soccer player, but peope noticed his greatness when he was still a boy.

Making a Name

Something absolutely terrible happened only one year after Ronaldinho started playing organized soccer. He was already proving himself on the pitch, playing with older boys and impressing everyone with a dizzying array of moves.

The young boy was only eight years old when his father suffered a heart attack while swimming in a pool and drowned.

Ronaldinho was devastated.

His father had been everything to him. He was his mentor, his soccer teacher, his playmate, his daddy. Now he was gone.

It was hard on everyone. Ronaldinho's mother would not be able to afford the family rent on her income alone, and his brother might even have to stop playing soccer and get a job.

Ronaldinho shut himself off from everyone for a little while and just concentrated on playing soccer and getting better every time his foot touched the ball. Surely things would have a way of working out, and as his father told him time and time again, "just keep things simple."

So he did.

And, eventually, things did begin to work out. In addition to his job at the shipyard, Ronaldinho's father

Being able to fake out defenders with his speed and agility, its easy for Ronaldinho to push the ball up near the opponent's goal.

used to work as a parking attendant for the local well-known soccer club —the Grêmio Football Club.

Ronaldinho's brother, Roberto, was a young player for the club, which was really more like an academy for young, very talented soccer players. The club thought so highly of Roberto and his family that they moved the family to a new house near the academy for free, as long as Roberto continued to play for them.

The family now lived in a rich part of town known as the Guarujá section of Porto Alegre.

They say that when one door closes another will open. And that is exactly what happened with Ronaldinho's family when it came to soccer. Everyone knew that his brother Roberto was destined for greatness. He was a superb football player. But he continued suffering one injury after another and eventually had to give up his dream of becoming one of the world's top soccer stars.

He tore his knee horribly and had to leave the club. He would eventually recover to play professional soccer for a few seasons in Sweden when he was older.

But now it was time for Roberto's younger brother, Ronaldinho, to make a name for himself on the soccer pitch. And he wouldn't disappoint.

The boy started training for four hours a day with Grêmio during the day and then would play two hours of futsal in the evenings with his friends.

"Ever since I was a little boy I just loved playing football," Ronaldinho the soccer star would later say. "It's a

Ronaldinho blasts a free kick that fooled the Lens' goalkeeper to give Paris Saint-Germain the lead.

gift that God gave me, and I'm just happy to be able to make a living out of it."

In fact, just about everyone in the area would know who Ronaldinho was when the boy was still only thirteen years old. Playing for a Grêmio youth team, Ronaldinho went on a scoring rampage and single-handedly scored 23 goals in one match that his team dominated 23–0!

There is some dispute as to whether this was an actual soccer match or a futsal match. It doesn't matter now because the newspapers and television reporters caught wind of the accomplishment and the youngster became an instant celebrity.

The young teenager didn't rely on his natural ability alone. In addition to hours of practice every single day, he spent lots of time studying some of the greatest Brazilian soccer players of all time.

He tried learning all he could about his nation's rich soccer history. He read about Brazil's heroic footballers, and he learned what they did to become great. If there was video or film, he studied it and tried to learn all he could. Ronaldinho was more than just a child prodigy; he was a student of the game.

The hard work paid off. In just a few short years, in 1997, Ronaldinho was called up to become part of the U-17 national team. This was a great honor and something that just about every sixteen-year-old soccer-playing boy in Brazil would wish for.

Ronaldinho was still considered to be one of the world's best—even when his team questioned his work ethic.

The squad travelled to Egypt to play in the FIFA U-17 World Cup. This was quite a culture shock for Ronaldinho and his teammates who had never been to that part of the world before. They were not used to the dry climate of North Africa and the Middle East. But they soon learned that soccer was played the same way anywhere there was a field.

Ronaldinho and his teammates stunned their first opponent, Austria, with a 7–0 whipping. Their second opponent was supposed to be much tougher. It was against a very strong United States team.

But Brazil's suffocating defense was too much, and they soared to a hard-fought 3–0 victory. They went on to beat Oman 3–1 to advance to the quarterfinals against Argentina.

Once again, Ronaldinho and the team buckled down defensively and won the match 2–0. They played Germany in the semifinals and again they did not allow a goal, winning 4–0.

With thrity-five thousand fans in attendance, Brazil fell behind to Ghana 1–0 late in the first half. It was the first time the team trailed during the entire tournament. The deficit would not last long. Brazil scored two goals in the second half to win the U-17 World Cup 2–1.

It wasn't long before Ronaldinho was called up to become part of the national team. But first, he would start getting offers to play professional soccer.

A dream was coming true.

chapter

4

Turning Pro

There was no doubt that Ronaldinho was a rising star. He was just one of those people that every fan in the stands seemed drawn to. When he was on the pitch, dribbling, passing, defending, or scoring he was just one of those players you had to watch.

He was a big deal in Brazilian soccer circles, and it wouldn't be long before the rest of the world noticed. The famous European clubs would soon start throwing millions of dollars at him to play in Europe.

It was right after Ronaldinho and his teammates won the U-17 FIFA World Cup in Egypt that the offers—at least from Brazilian teams—started coming in. He wasn't even eighteen years old when he signed his first contract, a deal with Grêmio.

How could he sign elsewhere? Grêmio had given both he and his brother their soccer starts. The brothers were practically raised by the club from the time they were young. Grêmio had also moved the family to a nice area and given them a new home. It didn't hurt that the club happened to be one of the most popular and powerful professional teams in all of Brazil.

Ronaldinho finds it important to be a great role model for children, so he takes any chance he gets to travel and play soccer with kids.

He made an immediate impact. His first professional appearance with the senior team was in the 1998 Copa Libertadores tournament. What captivated his coaches and teammates at the time was Ronaldinho's ability to create plays when cornered or when he appeared trapped. They said he was able to make something out of nothing, a skill that can probably be traced back to his futsal days where there is no room on the field to make a long pass. Instead, he would have to rely on his ball skills and on simply trying to outsmart his opponent.

"It's something that's a part of him," said famous former Brazilian soccer star Edinho, who coached Ronaldinho at Grêmio. "It's his nature to create new things during a game."

Another of his coaches at Grêmio, Antônio Lopes described the way Ronaldinho played as a beautiful combination of art and objectivity.

While his favorite Los Angeles Laker is Magic Johnson, Ronaldinho is very close friends with current Laker, Kobe Bryant.

Even though most people thought Ronaldinho was past his prime, he reestablished himself as an elite star while playing for Flamengo in 2011.

"When I managed him, one of the things that impressed me most was that he never wasted a dribble," Lopes said. "He could make tricks and pass defenders while trying to score a goal, all at the same time."

Another trait that separated him from other players—even the very good players—was that even though Ronaldinho was one of the best players on the pitch, he enjoyed passing the ball to his teammates. He found it thrilling to be able to make a pass and see one of his teammates score a goal or make a good play because of it.

He was the opposite of a ball hog, and some of this can be traced to his love of basketball and in particular his favorite all-time NBA player—Magic Johnson. Johnson, a Hall of Fame champion, was known as one of the most unselfish players in all of basketball during his years with the Los Angeles Lakers.

Even though he was one of the league's best scorers, Johnson always looked to pass the ball first and make the players around him even better. Ronaldinho admired him so much that he collected videotapes of Johnson's highlights and studied him whenever he had free time. He especially loved Johnson's "no-look" pass. This was when Johnson would anticipate where a player was going to be and then pass the ball to them without even looking in that direction.

Ronaldinho started doing the same thing on the pitch.

One of his future teammates, Henrik Larsson, would comment on Ronaldinho's uncanny knack for making the no-look pass or simply getting you the ball when you least expected it.

"I know that whenever I play and he's playing, I only need to make the runs," Larsson said about running toward open spaces without the ball. "There are not many runs you make that he misses. He always sees you. I always say that you have to be on the move whenever Ronaldinho gets the ball. Even when you don't expect to receive it, you can receive it. So you have to be on your toes all the time."

Ronaldinho excelled at Grêmio and for the Brazilian national team. After only a few years, it was pretty clear that his talent had exceeded expectations, and he had outgrown Grêmio. He was receiving offers from some of the very top clubs in Europe, but some had rules regarding

After being named the best Latin American soccer player in La Liga in 2004, Ronaldinho posed for pictures with his mother.

the number of international matches he had to play before becoming a part of their team.

So in 2001, he signed with a five-year contract with the French club Paris Saint-Germain that was worth millions of dollars. Ronaldinho was now a rich man. But because he didn't sign with one of the major teams like Barcelona, Arsenal, or Manchester United, his old team Grêmio received no compensation for him.

It is usual for the new team to pay a hefty sum of money to the player's old team—in this case Grêmio. Even though he did nothing wrong and followed the rules exactly, many Brazilian fans became angry with him.

That started what was a rocky time for him in France. Everything went great the first year there. Ronaldinho brought his family with him to live there, and he played very well, winning over French fans every time he played.

After winning the Copa Libertadores with Atlético Mineiro in 2013, Ronaldinho celebrates with the fans by blowing them kisses.

That was also the year that he helped Brazil win the World Cup, emerging as one of the greatest players in the world. He scored two goals in five games and assisted on many others as Brazil showed the world the concept of passing and true team play.

But it may have been a little too much for the young star. When he returned to France to play for Paris Saint-Germain, his attitude had changed. He seemed more interested in hanging out late and going to parties than he did playing soccer. The team kept him out of many games as he clashed with team manager Luis Fernández.

"He was very young when he came to Paris," Fernández said. "He wanted to learn, he wanted to work, he wanted to make progress. He came with his family, with his brother and his mother, and the first year went very well because he accepted that he had to work if he was going to develop. The second year was different because in the meantime he'd become the champion of the world. That can make a difference to the head of a player. You understand? He was still young, but now he thought he knew everything."

The clashes continued, and finally after only two seasons in France, Ronaldinho announced that he wanted to leave the club. Now there would be a bidding war to see who would get the young but now troubled player.

There was a lot of money at stake and so the question became: Would Ronaldinho rededicate himself to soccer?

European Superstar

If European soccer clubs were worried about Ronaldinho's commitment, they surely did not let it show. As soon as he announced that he wanted to leave Paris Saint-Germain, there was a bidding war for his services.

It came down to arguably the two richest clubs in the world. In the end, Barcelona outbid Manchester United and paid roughly $30 million to secure their newest star player.

He paid an immediate dividend, scoring a goal during his first game for Barcelona, a victory in what is known as a "friendly" match against AC Milan. A "friendly" is basically

At a young age, people knew Ronaldinho would become a star, but no one could have predicted him becoming one of the all-time greats.

After being named FIFA World Player of the Year in 2005, Ronaldinho poses with the second and third place winners of the award, Samuel Eto'o and Frank Lampard.

an exhibition match, usually against an international opponent that doesn't count in league play or in a specific tournament.

That season, Ronaldinho helped Barcelona finish in second place. Because of his talent and knack for both scoring and passing the ball, Ronaldinho played mainly in the midfield but was known as an attacking player. Many times the best players on the pitch are the midfielders. They may not score the most goals but they have the most responsibility on the field and control the speed and tempo of the match.

His next two seasons for Barcelona were nothing short of incredible. He dominated play in 2004, scoring 13 goals with 20 assists, followed by 26 goals and 22 assists the next season.

He was named the FIFA World Player of the Year both seasons, the highest honor any soccer player could earn. But it was the love of the fans that he cherished even more.

In November 2005, something historic happened. Barcelona traveled to Madrid to play their most hated and toughest rivals, Real Madrid, in a very important

Ronaldinho and Brazilian teammate, Rivaldo, celebrate by kissing the 2002 World Cup trophy after beating Germany for the championship.

tournament game. The winner would advance further while the losing team was eliminated. Ronaldinho was brilliant. He stopped Madrid's attacks in the midfield, created opportunities and attacks for his teammates all game, and even scored two goals to help Barcelona win the important match 3–0.

As Ronaldinho blew past two defenders running down the left side, he started angling toward the keeper, who moved over to defend against a left-footed blast. But it never came. Instead, Ronaldinho tapped a slow shot with his right foot into the far corner of the net. His teammates mobbed him and celebrated the game-clinching goal.

That's when the unthinkable happened. The Real Madrid fans who had packed the stadium stood and cheered, giving Ronaldinho—a player from the other team—a standing ovation. Only once before in history had a visiting player been given a standing ovation, and that was for soccer legend Diego Maradona.

"It was a perfect game," Ronaldinho said. "I will never forget this because it is very rare for any footballer to be applauded in this way by the opposition fans."

What he did in Barcelona was remarkable. Almost singlehandedly, Ronaldinho helped take a team that had been struggling and put it back on top. During his time there he helped lead Barcelona to two Spanish La Liga titles and one UEFA Champions League title.

Years later, this prompted Barcelona goalkeeper Víctor Valdés—who played with many all-time great players

While playing for AC Milan, Ronaldinho had the chance to play against American soccer star Landon Donovan.

After beating Espanyol for the 2006 Spanish Supercup, Ronaldinho walks off the pitch with the trophy and teammates Lilian Thuram, and Gianluca Zambrotta.

including Lionel Messi—to proclaim Ronaldinho as the greatest player he ever shared the field with.

"I have always said that 'Rony' changed the club's history when he played at Barca. He was the leader of that team which changed [our] history," Valdés said. "We had not won any title for many years. He arrived and powered Barcelona to become a club known worldwide. And that alone is a reason to thank him. I would say he is the biggest talent I have seen."

But Ronaldinho always had dreams of playing for some of the other famous clubs in Europe. So, when his contract with Barcelona expired, the star announced that he needed a new challenge. He soon signed with Italian superpower AC Milan.

But even though he was still relatively young, Ronaldinho's body started breaking down a bit. Injuries caused him to struggle for his first season and half in Milan. By the end of his second season, he had regained his form and was among the league leaders in assists.

Still, his performance was not the same as it was in Barcelona and he was even left off of Brazil's 2010 World Cup team.

Ronaldinho lasted only three seasons in Milan and decided that the best way to show the world he could still play was to go home and play in Brazil. He joined Flamengo and instantly led the team to a championship. He reestablished himself by scoring 21 goals and notching 8 assists during the 2011 season.

Things soured, though, and the next season he quit the team claiming the club had not paid him in months.

He joined another club, Atlético Mineiro, but really only had one thing in mind. He completed the 2012 season with Mineiro, then signed an extension to remain with the club through 2013. In the past two seasons, Ronaldinho has shown the world that he still has the skills to be among the best in the sport. But what he really wants is a shot at making the Brazilian national team and competing in the 2014 World Cup.

chapter 6

More than Soccer

Ronaldinho has accomplished just about everything someone can in soccer. He played on the biggest world stages, playing for Barcelona and AC Milan, competing in the Olympics, and even winning the coveted World Cup.

He has been adored worldwide and even cheered at opponent's stadiums. But despite all of the fame and the incredible career, those closest to him say he has not changed a bit from the boy who grew up in humble surroundings in Brazil.

His brother acts as his manager. His sister, Deisi, serves as his press secretary and even a cousin—Tiago—is his

When Flamengo signed Ronaldinho, he felt it was a chance to prove to the world that he should still be considered a superstar.

driver. Ronaldinho hates driving and has pretty much stopped doing it all together.

The three family members are usually with Ronaldinho wherever he lives, often sharing a big home with him whether it is in Spain, Italy, or back home in Brazil.

He also remains very close to his mother and flies her out to see him usually four to five times a year for month-long visits. When they are together, she makes sure that she cooks her son's favorite dishes.

"His favorite foods are rice, beans, barbecued meat, and pasta," she said during a rare behind-the-scenes documentary called *Ronaldinho: A Day in the Life of...* .

In addition to his small, close-knit family, Ronaldinho regularly flies dozens of his closest friends to spend time with him wherever he is living. They spend time grilling, going to the beaches, and listening to music.

"I love to listen to music, all types of music," Ronaldinho said. "But my favorite type of music is samba."

Several of his longtime friends have commented that Ronaldinho has never let fame or money change who he is. He is the same kid that used to play futsal with them when they were younger. The superstar does not like living in big, crowded cities. Instead, he chooses to live in the suburbs, away from the crowds and the noise.

"I love living near the mountains and the beach," he said.

But besides enjoying good times with close friends, there is another more serious side to Ronaldinho. In particular, there is an issue that he feels very strongly about and has spent a lot of energy fighting it: racism.

Unfortunately, racism is a big problem during European soccer matches. Many fans look down on players with dark skin and shout and chant terrible names at them. This has caused some players to walk off the pitch right in the middle of games in protest.

Ronaldinho himself has been the target of such cruel attacks. He sponsored an anti-racism game to raise awareness with his friend and former teammate Lionel Messi. The two served as captains for their teams and wowed fans by playing to a 7–7 tie.

"Racism is a very serious matter. We are constantly trying to get the message across that it is wrong," he said. I would say look at the other side to it; people are the same, irrespective of the color of their skin, their race or whatever else. I'd like to say that racism is not the right way. Going to the stadium to have fun and support your team—to be happy. That's the right way."

He has also appeared in various television and YouTube commercials promoting tolerance and speaking out against racism. But perhaps one of the most important things he did was just a simple, yet very powerful, hug.

One of Barcelona's greatest players was an African by the name of Samuel Eto'o. Both he and Ronaldinho teamed up on numerous goals over the years. The European fans were being especially rough on Eto'o, calling him names

When Ronaldinho joined Atlético Mineiro in 2012, he changed the organization for the better and started getting back into his old habit of scoring a lot.

and throwing bananas at him on the field. He told the referee that he had enough and was walking off.

Ronaldinho stopped him. He talked the player into staying. He told him the best way to shut up the fans would be to play great and win the game against their team.

He listened and stayed. A little while later, Ronaldinho scored a goal on a free kick. Instead of his usual celebration, he ran over to Eto'o and hugged his teammate for a very long time, showing the fans that the players were united regardless of the color of his skin.

It was a great moment and since then many other soccer stars have spoken out against racism in the sport. A Nike campaign ensued called "Stand Up, Speak Out," against racism.

Today, Ronaldinho continues playing soccer, and is working hard to earn another spot on the World Cup stage. But even if his career was to end sooner than he would like, the Brazilian with the long hair and the wide smile would have to be listed among the greatest who ever played the game.

Career Highlights and Awards

- Copa América champion: 1999
- FIFA Confederations Cup Golden Ball: 1999
- FIFA Confederations Cup Golden Shoe: 1999
- UEFA Intertoto Cup champion (with Paris Saint-Germain): 2001
- FIFA World Cup champion: 2002
- FIFA World Cup All-Star Team: 2002
- Don Balón Award: 2003–04, 2005–06
- UEFA Club Best Forward: 2004–05
- La Liga champion (with Barcelona): 2004–05, 2005–06
- FIFPro World XI: 2005, 2006, 2007
- FIFA World Player of the Year: 2004, 2005
- FIFA Confederations Cup champion: 2005
- Ballon d'Or: 2005
- Supercopa de España (with Barcelona): 2005, 2006
- FIFPro World Player of the Year: 2005, 2006
- UEFA Club Footballer of the Year: 2005–06
- UEFA Champions League champion (with Barcelona): 2005–06

- Olympic Bronze Medal: 2008
- Golden Foot award: 2009
- Campeonato Carioca champion (with Flamengo): 2011
- Superclásico de las Américas champion: 2011
- Bola de Ouro award: 2012
- Campeonato Mineiro champion (with Atlético Mineiro): 2013
- Copa Libertadores champion (with Atlético Mineiro): 2013
- Won an ESPY award for Best Soccer Player in 2006.
- Scored 110 goals in 250 games with Barcelona.

INTERNET ADDRESSES

Official Atlético Mineiro Webpage

<http://www.atletico.com.br/site/>

Official Facebook Page

<https://www.facebook.com/RonaldinhoOficial>

FIFA Official Site

<http://www.fifa.com/>

INDEX